Brown Rabbit's Shape Book

Alan Baker

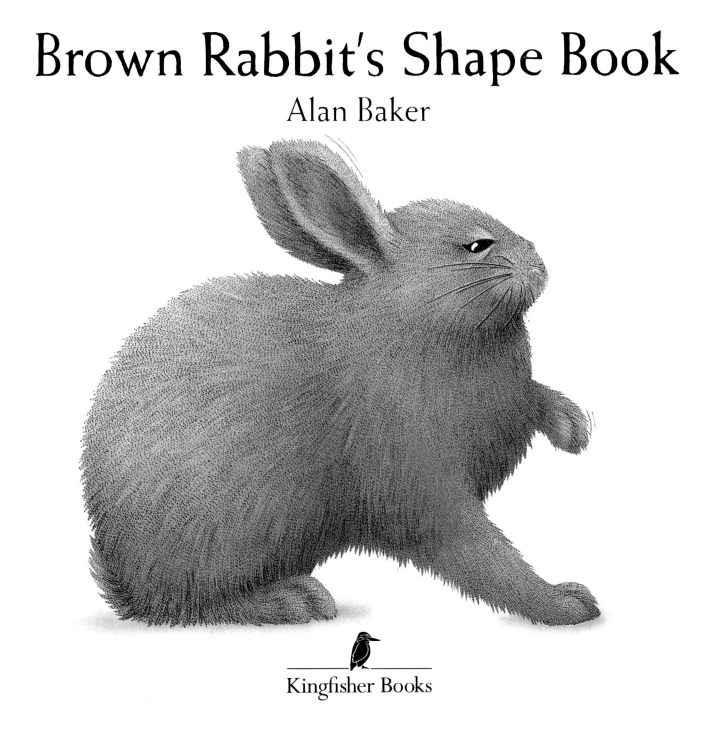

Kingfisher Books

Kingfisher Books, Grisewood & Dempsey Ltd,
Elsley House, 24-30 Great Titchfield Street,
London W1P 7AD

First published in 1994 by Kingfisher Books
10 9 8 7 6 5 4 3 2 1

BRITISH LIBRARY CATALOGUING IN
PUBLICATION DATA
A catalogue record for this book is available
from the British Library

ISBN 1 85697 181 3

Cover designed by Caroline Johnson
Phototypeset by Southern Positives and
Negatives (SPAN), Lingfield, Surrey
Printed in Singapore

One day a parcel arrived
for Brown Rabbit.
It had bright red triangles
on the wrapping paper.

The card was
the shape of a
rectangle. It said
"To Brown Rabbit".

To Brown x
Rabbit xx

Rabbit took off the paper.
Underneath was a
square box. Rabbit
lifted the lid.

Inside was
a tube ...

... with a circle shape top.
Rabbit opened it.

Out tumbled
five flat floppy
balloons,
all different
colours.

Lovely balloons,
just waiting
to be blown up.

Rabbit blew up the red balloon.
It was big and round like a ball.

Whoosh! away it flew.

The orange balloon was
oval-shaped like an egg.

Whoosh! It flew off.

The green balloon was l o n g
and sausage-shaped.
Rabbit couldn't hold it.
Whoo-whoosh!
Off it went.

The purple balloon
was smaller and
shaped like a pear.

One more puff, thought Rabbit.
Then BANG! It burst.

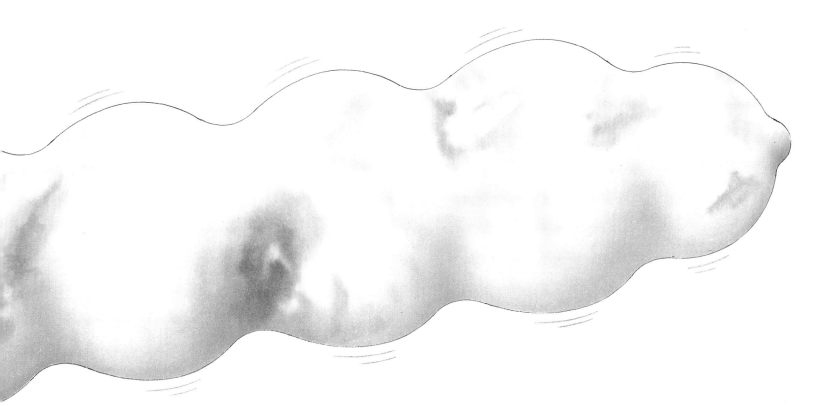

The last balloon was all colours,
l o n g and lumpy-bumpy.

Whoosh! Blast off!

Whoo ... Whoo ... Whoo-oosh!

Goodbye balloon shapes.
I'm all out of puff,
thought Rabbit

He tidied up the balloons,
the tube, the box
and the paper.

Then rabbit-shaped Rabbit
fell fast asleep on top.